SNOW WHITE
And the Seven Dwarfs

**A Page to Panto script
by
Joe Meloy**

FROM THE PAGE TO MAGIC ON THE STAGE!

Beercott

Snow white and the Seven Dwarfs.
A pantomime in 2 acts

First Published in Great Britain in 2023 by Beercott Books.

Copyright: © Joe Meloy 2023

ISBN:978-1-7393020-3-0

Joe Meloy has asserted his rights to be identified
as the author of this book.

Title is fully protected under copyright. All rights, including professional and amateur stage production, recitation, lecturing, public reading, motion picture, radio broadcasting, television and the rights of translation into foreign languages are strictly reserved.

A catalogue record of this book is available from the British Library.

No one shall make any changes to the play for the purpose of production. No part of this book may be reproduced, stored in a retrieval system, or transmitted in any form, by any means, now known or yet to be invented. This includes mechanical, electronic, photocopying, recording, videotaping, or otherwise, without the prior written permission of the publisher. No one shall upload this title, or part of this title, to social media websites.

Professional and amateur producers are hereby warned that title is subject to a licencing fee. Publication of this play does not imply availability for performance. Both amateurs and professionals considering a production are strongly advised to apply to the agent before starting rehearsals, advertising, or booking a theatre. A licence fee must be paid whether the title is presented for charity or gain and whether or not admission is charged.

Worldwide licence enquiries for this title should be directed to:
licencing@beercottbooks.co.uk.
Title subject to availability.

---

www.beercottbooks.co.uk

For my Mum, Dawn.

Love you always.

CHARACTERS

SNOW WHITE - The lead character of the pantomime. A Pantomime princess.

MUDDLES (COMIC) - Snow White's best friend and the Queen's jester.

DAME MAISY MARMALADE (DAME) - The Queen's cook, Nanny to Snow White and Mother to Muddles.

RAMSBOTTOM - The Queen's Henchman with a heart of gold, who wouldn't hurt a fly.

THE WICKED QUEEN (BADDIE) - The villain of the piece thoroughly evil and rotten to the core!

MAGIC MIRROR - A walk talking Magic Mirror, who can be a bit sassy.

PRINCE FREDERICK - The handsome Prince, as charming as he is handsome.

THE SEVEN DWARFS - Pop, Jolly, Surly, Dozy, Wheezy, Blusher and Snoozy. They live in a little cottage in the forest and work in the diamond mine

CHORUS PLAYING THE VARIOUS ROLES - Villagers, Minions, Stylists, Servants, School Children and even forest animals!

SCENES

ACT 1

PROLOGUE

SCENE 1 - The Royal Palace

SCENE 2 - The Royal Palace

SCENE 3 - The Royal Palace

SCENE 4 - The Forest

SCENE 5 - The Royal Palace

SCENE 6 - the Dwarf's Cottage

ACT 2

SCENE 1 - The Diamond Mine

SCENE 2 - The Royal Palace

SCENE 3 - The Royal Palace

SCENE 4 - The Royal Palace

SCENE 5 - The Forest

SCENE 6 - The Dwarf's Cottage

SCENE 7 - The Dwarf's Cottage

SCENE 8 - The Royal Palace

SCENE 9 - Song Sheet

SCENE 10 - Bows.

ACT ONE PROLOGUE

(Enter the MAGIC MIRROR)

MIRROR: Good evening one and all,
 I'm the Magic Mirror on the Wall,
 Tonight I have quite the story to tell you all!
 We have a very handsome Prince,
 We also have an Evil Queen, a nasty site to be seen
 Our Queen is self-obsessed and rotten,
 So vein, taking selfies, posting to insta, she'd hate to be forgotten
 There are others as well both bold and bright,
 A silly Jester, a henchman and of course Snow White
 There's a story about to begin,
 To the Royal Kingdom where the party is in full swing!

(Enter EVIL QUEEN)

QUEEN: Just one minute you shiny piece of glass!
 Don't move a muscle, stay right there and not so fast!
 Actually hold on, the lighting is just right, *(takes out her phone)*
 I've just had my lips done and my smile looks bright! *(Takes a selfie)*
 I'll never grow old I'm totally glam,
 Don't you forget that boys and girls; Oh yes I am!

(AUDIENCE: Oh no you're not!)

OH YES I AM!

(AUDIENCE: Oh no you're not!)

OH YES I AM!

(AUDIENCE: Oh no you're not!)

I'm the boss around here, the Queen, I'm gorgeous, lovely-

MIRROR: -And very mean!

QUEEN: Silence! Now then magic mirror, let me ask you this!
 Tell me truthfully and don't you dare be remiss
 Mirror Mirror on the wall, who's the fairest of them all?

MIRROR: She's beautiful, radiant and kind to her core,
 You are not the fairest in the land anymore!

QUEEN: What?!

MIRROR: It is your stepdaughter Snow White,
 So young, so beautiful and oh so bright

QUEEN: Silence mirror! I've heard enough!

> *(Exit MIRROR)...*
>
> *(Looking out at the audience)* Ugh! What a vile looking lot, no wonder we're here in *(local reference)*, you know they only built *(local reference)* to keep the riff raff out of Frinton! If you're going to boo me, you may as well do it properly you snivelling butch of seaside chavs! Yes, that's it lovely I love my boo's! I knew I should have gotten rid of Snow White when I disposed of her Father after I married him, everything that little brat has done has got in my way! And now she's apparently prettier than me? Well, we'll soon see. I've invited the gorgeous Prince Fredrick to the Palace and just watch as he decides I am to become his bride! He'll choose me won't he boys and girls, as I'm the most beautiful woman in the land! Oh yes I am!
>
> *(AUDIENCE: oh no you're not!)*
>
> Oh yes I am!
>
> *(AUDIENCE: oh no you're not!)*
>
> Oh yes I am!
>
> *(AUDIENCE: oh no you're not!).*
>
> Oh shut up you pathetic lot... Hang on a minute I can smell something... Urgh! It's children, I hate children! They're horrible, if it were up to me children would be banned from public! And look at all the adults here, you're no better coming to watch a pantomime! Grow up the lot of you! *(Evil Laugh. Exit QUEEN)*

ACT 1 — SNOW WHITE — 11

SCENE ONE

THE ROYAL PALACE

(The lights come up full on the kingdom as everyone enters in full party mode. SNOW WHITE leads the opening number)

Song One – SNOW WHITE & ENSEMBLE

(Song Ends. SNOW WHITE is centre)

SNOW WHITE: Oh, I do love singing and dancing with you all!

QUEEN: *(Offstage)* Snow White! It's time to do your chores!

VILLAGER 1: Why do you do what that nasty woman says Snow White?

SNOW WHITE: Because she's my stepmother and ever since Father died, she's in charge. And besides it's not that bad, all I have to do today is; hoover the palace, dust the shelves, collect the groceries, bathe the palace guard dogs, clean out the horses stables, sort through all of the mail, update the Queen's Facebook, Twitter, Instagram, TikTok and Snap Chat to make sure in her words she 'stays relevant', clean all of the dishes, make lunch and dinner, re-carpet the stairs, paint all of the palace pillars and make all of the beds. See it's not much.

VILLAGER 2: I wish you'd just stand up to her Snow White

SNOW WHITE: She's far too scary! Besides she'll get her comeuppance, I'm sure!

QUEEN: *(From offstage)* SNOW WHITE! CHORES NOW!

SNOW WHITE: Quickly everyone you must leave, and I've got to go, she's growing impatient! *(Exit off SNOW WHITE and ensemble)*

(Enter MUDDLES)

MUDDLES: Hiya everyone my name is Muddles, and I'm the Queen's jester so it's my job to cheer her up and make her laugh, which if you've met her, you know isn't an easy task. As well as the jester around here I'm also the cook, cleaner, flower arranger, butler and everything else. The Queen would have me gone, but I'm still here as me and my Mum promised the King before he died that we'd stick around and help look after Snow White. I'm sure you'll meet my Mum at some point, apparently I take after her with broad shoulders, deep voice and a hairy back… We've lived in this big castle for years, my Mum tells me we've been here for generations. I became a jester because Mum tells me that my Dad was a jester, she also said he could have been a cook, cleaner, butler, milkman or a postman... I always wondered why he had so many jobs! That's probably why I took on lots of jobs around here! I do love living here, but only because of Snow White, she makes the world go round and my heart flutter! In fact I'll tell you a secret... I fancy Snow White! She's so beautiful and kind! *(Sighs)*. Here hang on a second I've actually written some new royal jokes for the Queen, would you like to hear them? Well then here goes; What did one royal family member say to the other before getting in a fight? Put your dukes up! Trust me, the jokes don't get any better! I always like to hold the door open for people, as a nice; jester... Do you know, I've never seen a royal flush. Then again, I've never been in the Queen's bathroom! It's alright I'll keep working on them, I mean they can't get any worse! Here I've got a great idea, do you all fancy being my friends? *(Ad lib as needed)* great well when I come onstage, I'm going to come on and say, Hiya Gang! And you shout back 'Hiya Muddles!' Shall we give it a go? *(Ad lib as needed)* Right I'm going off! Ready? *(goes off)* Hiya Gang!

(AUDIENCE: Hiya Muddles!)

Did you say anything? You did well let's try it again then! *(goes off)* Hiya Gang!

(AUDIENCE: Hiya Muddles!)

Oh, great that's more like it! I'm so glad we're all friends!

(The intro to song two begins)

That'll be my Mum, she does like to make an entrance! Ladies and Gentlemen of the Royal Court please welcome the ever elegant, the glamorous- Who wrote this?

DAME: *(From offstage)* Keep reading!

MUDDLES: Who doesn't look a day over twenty-one- Really? My Mum Dame Maisy Marmalade!

Song Two – Lady Marmalade – DAME MAISY MARMALADE

Hey Sister, Go Sister, Soul Sister, Go Sister Hey Sister, Go Sister, Soul Sister, Go Sister

(DAME enters with bags of shopping from Tesco)

You meet Marmalade down in old *(local reference)* Town Struttin' my stuff in the isles

I'll say 'Hello,

Tesco, you wanna gimme some discount? Mmm, mmm

Buy one get one free for teatime Buy one get one free for teatime Mocha-choca-lattes on offer

Call me Maisy Marmalade

Bonjour je m'appelle I'm Maisy! Maisy! Bonjour je m'appelle I'm Maisy!

I went to the Tesco's near McDs freshened up I got lots of sweet treats with my club card

On the tills there was a spill, clean up on isle twelve

Buy one get one free for teatime Buy one get one free for teatime Mocha-choca-lattes on offer

Call me Maisy Marmalade

Bonjour je m'appelle I'm Maisy! Maisy! Bonjour je m'appelle I'm Maisy!

(Spoken) For those that don't speak French that's hello my name is Maisy… I know I'm so elegant and so refined. And I've also got some sweeties from Tesco! Who wants some sweeties? *(DAME throws out sweets to the audience. Adlib as needed)*

Hey, hey, hey

Touching my skin feelin' silky smooth That's Tesco's anti-aging cream

Can't believe these bags are 20p More, more, more

Now I'm at home scrubbing all these pots Living this old boring life

But when I go off to shop

This girl starts to bop, more, more, more

Buy one get one free for teatime Buy one get one free for teatime Mocha-choca-lattes on offer

Call me Maisy Marmalade

Bonjour je m'appelle I'm Maisy! Maisy! Bonjour je m'appelle

I'm Maisy!

Bonjour je m'appelle I'm Maisy! Maisy! Bonjour je m'appelle I'm Maisy!

Buy one get one free for teatime Buy one get one free for teatime Mocha-choca-lattes on offer

Call me Maisy Marmalade

DAME: Oh, Hello boys and girls! I'm sure we can do better than that! Hello Everyone! That's much better! What a lovely looking lot we've got in tonight! Honestly, you're the best audience we've had in tonight! Do you like my frock boys and girls? It's my special American dress, one yank and it's off! Well, how silly of me boys and girls I haven't introduced myself, my name is Dame Maisy-Daisy-Lolly Wally-Dora-Mora-Smith-Smith-ington-Smily-Whiley-Do-Dah-Green-Von-Mon-Don-How-You-Doing- There-Son the third Marmalade, but you can all just call me Maisy! *(pointing to a man on the front row)* and you can call me anytime you like! I'm the head cook here for the Queen and Nanny to the beautiful Snow White, I cook up all of the royal meals. But I almost forgot, I've got some rather exciting news, I've met a man, yes, he'll be my fourth husband; My first husband was a human cannonball, oh he was so brave and the day he was fired was the day he died... Then there was my second husband who was a milk man he loved to bathe in milk, one day he asked me to fill his bath for him and I said how do you want it? and he said pasteurised, and he drowned... Then my third husband, ooh he was lovely, but he met a terrible end, he fell into a vat of Varnish, but he did have a lovely finish. And my fourth husband *(back to the man she picked on before)* hello gorgeous! I'm about to make you get every penny of your tickets worth tonight! *(adlib with the man on the front row where he's from etc)* Right I've made this man's evening, we can get back to it-

(Enter PRINCE FREDERICK)

PRINCE: Excuse me Sir?

DAME: Sir? I'm a woman!

PRINCE: Yes, I can see that now, I'm here to meet the Queen!

DAME: Best of luck... Why are you meeting the Queen?

PRINCE: She is to be my bride and I am to become King!

ACT 1 SNOW WHITE 15

DAME: You've not met the Queen yet have you?

PRINCE: No, but I'm assured she is kind, sweet and beautiful through and through.

(Enter SNOW WHITE)

You must be the Queen, you were right you are beautiful!

SNOW WHITE: Oh, I'm not the Queen-

PRINCE: But you must be, you look like royalty to me-

SNOW WHITE: The Queen is my stepmother

PRINCE: Oh. I'm supposed to be meeting the Queen to marry her-

SNOW WHITE: But she's so much older than you-

DAME: Yeah, and she's horrible!

SNOW WHITE: Maisy! You needn't be so mean!

DAME: I'm only telling the truth and I can see Prince Fredrick only has eyes for you!

SNOW WHITE: He's only been here five minutes!

PRINCE: It's true. The second I saw you; you took my breath away.

DAME: Oh, I can feel a song coming on! *(Exit DAME)*

Song Three – PRINCE & SNOW WHITE

(Song Ends, SNOW WHITE and THE PRINCE kiss. A Royal fanfare is heard)

SNOW WHITE: Oh, that sounds like the Queen's on her way! I've got to go!

PRINCE: But will I ever see you again?

SNOW WHITE: Of course you will, true love always finds a way!

(Exit SNOW WHITE. Enter QUEEN)

QUEEN: *(Aside)* Hello boys and girls did you miss me? Oh shut up! I'm here to meet my new husband! And there he is; Prince Frederick. He's a much younger man, but I don't look a day over twenty-one! So I assume he'll fall instantly in love with me! Hang on the lighting in here is sooooooo on fleek. *(takes out her phone)* hashtag Insta ready! Hashtag no filter needed. I look stunning. *(Spotting PRINCE FREDERICK)*. There he is Prince

Frederick, let me just check myself in my magic mirror selfie app *(checks herself out in her phone)*. As I thought I'm such a beautiful woman, Instagram is lucky to have someone as stunning as me grace it with my presence! Prince Frederick, you're as handsome as you described! I cannot wait to spend the rest of our lives together ruling side by side! Come here you may kiss my hand. *(Pulls PRINCE in for a selfie)*. Our first photo together as a couple, we look amazing! Now let me just caption this and send it for the world to see! Hashtag my world, hashtag new hubby, ring emoji, world emoji and the love heart emoji. This post is going to set social media on fire! I'm so happy you swiped right for me babes. Now what size suit are you?

PRINCE: I don't know, but-

QUEEN: Never mind, I have a team of onsite stylists *(QUEEN claps her hands and a group of STYLISTS come on and start measuring the PRINCE for his new suit)*. Yes, I think you'll look marvellous in a full white suit, and I your beautiful bride in a pure white silk gown-

PRINCE: But I don't want to marry you-

(STYLISTS recoil in horror. One faints.)

QUEEN: What did you say?

PRINCE: I said I don't want to marry you.

QUEEN: Why ever not? You'd go viral across all the socials and I've got a deal setup with 'Okay' magazine for the rights to our royal wedding.

PRINCE: Because I'm not in love with you, and also I think you might be old enough to be my Mum.

(STYLISTS gasp)

QUEEN: How dare you I don't look a day over twenty-one!

PRINCE: Oh yes you do!

QUEEN: Oh no I don't!

PRINCE: Oh yes you do!

QUEEN: Oh no I don't!

PRINCE: Oh yes you do!

ACT 1   SNOW WHITE   17

QUEEN: Oh no I don't!

PRINCE: Oh yes you do!

QUEEN: Oh, Shut up!

PRINCE: Besides, I think you should marry for love.

QUEEN: What has love got to do with getting married! And you'd have so many followers on Insta, TikTok and of course you'd have a Facebook page of likes-

PRINCE: I'm not on social media-

(STYLISTS gasp again)

Will you lot be quiet! In fact all of you go away!

STYLIST 1: I think we'd rather stay here

QUEEN: Do you know I think I saw someone out there wearing Adidas jogging bottoms...

STYLIST 2: Jogging bottoms?!

STYLIST 1: Not in this kingdom!

(STYLISTS exit in a hurry)

QUEEN: Now then, if you marry me, you'd be King and live a life of luxury!

PRINCE: But when you fall in love that is the luxury. To be loved and cared for by someone who loves you back is incredible. And besides I'm already in love with Snow White, so you'd become my Mother-in- law-

QUEEN: Snow White?!

PRINCE: Yes, it was love at first site.

QUEEN: Why would you want to marry that, when you can have all of this?

PRINCE: Will you give me your blessing to marry your stepdaughter?

QUEEN: You will never have my blessing! I bring you here to become my husband and you choose that ugly troll over me! Guards! *(enter GUARDS)* Take Prince Frederick deep into the forest where he will be banished forever more! And rest assured my boy you will never see Snow White again!

(GUARDS drag PRINCE FREDERICK away)

PRINCE: You won't get away with this! *(Exit PRINCE and GUARDS)*

(Blackout)

ACT 1 — SNOW WHITE — 19

SCENE TWO

THE ROYAL PALACE

MUDDLES: Hiya Gang! *(Audience: Hiya Muddles)*

DAME: Come along Muddles we've got to deliver these letters for the Queen

MUDDLES: Well can you help me with it Mum I'm so confused

DAME: It doesn't take much-

MUDDLES: I'm trying to address these letters to the right people, but I can't remember where people live.

DAME: No problem tell me what you've got so far.

MUDDLES: I don't know where to start-

DAME: *(Takes the letters off MUDDLES)* Right let me have a look. Ah right then it's quite easy. Now then Who lives in the first house, What's in the second house and I Don't Know lives in the third house

MUDDLES: That's what I want to find out.

DAME: I told you; Who's in the first, What's in the second, I Don't Know's in the third.

MUDDLES: Are you the manager?

DAME: I'm the postman!

MUDDLES: Woman.

DAME: Yes, postwoman thank you.

MUDDLES: So, you're in charge then?

DAME: Yes.

MUDDLES: And you don't know the blokes' names?

DAME: Well, I suppose I should.

MUDDLES: Well then who's in the first house?

DAME: Yes.

MUDDLES: I mean the person's name.

DAME: Who.

MUDDLES: The guy in the first house.

DAME: Who.

MUDDLES: The first person's house.

DAME: Who.

MUDDLES: The person living in the first house...

DAME: Who is in the first house!

MUDDLES: I'm asking YOU who's in the first house.

DAME: That's the man's name.

MUDDLES: That's who's name?

DAME: Yes.

MUDDLES: Well go ahead and tell me.

DAME: That's it.

MUDDLES: That's who?

DAME: Yes.

MUDDLES: Look, you've got a first house?

DAME: I have indeed

MUDDLES: Who's in the first house?

DAME: That's right.

MUDDLES: When you post the first letter, who gets it?

DAME: He does.

MUDDLES: All I'm trying to find out is, the name of the man, who is in the first house!

DAME: Who.

MUDDLES: The guy that lives in the first house!

DAME: Who.

MUDDLES: So, who gets the letter?

DAME: He does, every word of it. Sometimes his wife comes down and collects it.

MUDDLES: Who's wife?

DAME: Yes, what's wrong with that?

MUDDLES: Look, all I want to know is when the first person, from the first house has a special delivery how does he sign for it, how does he sign his name?

DAME: Who.

MUDDLES: The person in the first house.

DAME: Who.

MUDDLES: How does he sign-

DAME: That's how he signs it.

MUDDLES: Who?

DAME: Yes.

MUDDLES: All I'm trying to find out is what's the bloke's name in the first house!

DAME: No. What is in the second house

MUDDLES: I'm not asking you who's in the second house.

DAME: Who's in the first house.

MUDDLES: One person at a time!

DAME: Well, don't change the houses then!

MUDDLES: I'm not changing anything!

DAME: Look Muddles, just take some deep breaths and calm down!

MUDDLES: I'm only asking you, who's the guy in the first house!

DAME: That's right.

MUDDLES: Ok.

DAME: Alright.

MUDDLES: What's the man's name in the first house?

DAME: No. What is in the second house.

MUDDLES: I'm not asking you who's in the second house.

DAME: Who's in the first house.

MUDDLES: I don't know.

DAME: Well he's in the third house and we're not talking about him.

MUDDLES: Now how did I get onto the third house?

DAME: You mentioned his name.

MUDDLES: If I mentioned the third person's name, who did I say is living in the third house?

DAME: No. Who's in the first house.

MUDDLES: What's in first house?

DAME: What's in the second house.

MUDDLES: I don't know.

DAME: He's in the third house.

MUDDLES: Would you just stay on the third house, and don't go off them.

DAME: All right, what do you want to know?

MUDDLES: Now who's in the third house?

DAME: Why do you insist on who being in the third house?

MUDDLES: What is in the third house?

DAME: No. What is in the second house.

MUDDLES: You don't want who in the second house?

DAME: Who is in the first house.

MUDDLES: I don't know. Maybe you should think about the other houses?

DAME: Sure.

MUDDLES: The person living in the fourth houses name?

DAME: Why.

MUDDLES: I just thought I'd ask you.

DAME: Well, I just thought I'd tell you

MUDDLES: Then tell me who's in the fourth house.

DAME: Who's in the first house.

MUDDLES: Let me make this really simple; I want to know, what is the person's name in the fourth house?

DAME: No, What is in the second house.

MUDDLES: I'm not asking you who's in the second house.

DAME: Who's in the first house!

MUDDLES: I don't know the fourth person's name?

DAME: Why.

MUDDLES: Because!

DAME: Oh, he's in the fifth house

MUDDLES: Look, let's move on, have you got a sixth house?

DAME: Sure.

MUDDLES: The person living in the sixth house's name?

DAME: Tomorrow.

MUDDLES: You don't want to tell me today?

DAME: I'm telling you now.

MUDDLES: Then go ahead.

DAME: Tomorrow!

MUDDLES: What time?

DAME: What do you mean what time?

MUDDLES: What time tomorrow are you going to tell me who's living in the sixth house?

DAME: Now listen. Who is not living in the sixth house.

MUDDLES: I want to know what's living in the sixth house?

DAME: What's in the second house.

MUDDLES: I don't know. Have you got another house?

DAME: I have indeed.

MUDDLES: Then what's his name in the seventh house?

DAME: Today.

MUDDLES: Today, and tomorrow's in the sixth house.

DAME: Now you've got it.

MUDDLES: All we've got is a couple of hours to deliver these letters. You know I'm a postman too, I can deliver letters as well.

DAME: So, you tell me.

MUDDLES: I get up to the first house and deliver the first letter, I knock on the door and who answers the door?

DAME: Now that's the first thing you've said right.

MUDDLES: I don't even know what I'm talking about!

DAME: That's all you have to do.

MUDDLES: All I have to do is deliver the first letter

DAME: Yes!

MUDDLES: So who's first?

DAME: Naturally.

MUDDLES: Look, if I deliver the first letter, somebody's got to be delivered to first, get it? Now who is it?

DAME: Naturally.

MUDDLES: Who?

DAME: Naturally.

MUDDLES: Naturally?

DAME: Naturally.

MUDDLES: So, I post the letter to the first person who is Naturally.

DAME: No, you don't, you post it to Who.

MUDDLES: Naturally.

DAME: That's different.

MUDDLES: That's what I said.

DAME: You're not saying it...

MUDDLES: I post it to Naturally.

DAME: You post it to Who.

MUDDLES: Naturally.

DAME: That's it.

MUDDLES: That's what I said!

DAME: You ask me.

MUDDLES: I post it to who?

DAME: Naturally.

MUDDLES: Now you ask me.

DAME: You post it to Who?

MUDDLES: Naturally.

DAME: That's it.

MUDDLES: So, I think I've got it; Who's in the first house, What's second, I Don't Know's third, Why's fourth, in the fifth house Today, Because is sixth and the final house is Tomorrow!

DAME: What?

MUDDLES: Let's not start all that again!

(Blackout)

SCENE THREE
THE ROYAL PALACE

QUEEN: It's me again. *(Evil laugh)* Did you miss me? So that stupid Prince wants to marry that silly girl Snow White, well I'll make sure she'll never steal another man from me again! Ramsbottom!

(Enter RAMSBOTTOM, the Queen's Henchman)

RAMSBOTTOM: Yes, ma 'lady?

QUEEN: I have a job for you.

RAMSBOTTOM: A job your majesty? What kind of job?

QUEEN: The most important job. I need you to take Snow White to the depths of the forest.

RAMSBOTTOM: And play a game of I-spy!

QUEEN: No! Listen-

RAMSBOTTOM: Or maybe we could have a picnic… I could bring scotch eggs!

QUEEN: Silence you bumbling imbecile! You will take Snow White to the depths of the forest and kill her!

RAMSBOTTOM: What, dead your majesty?!

QUEEN: Yes. I want her dead. She has stolen Prince Frederick from me!

RAMSBOTTOM: I don't know your majesty-

QUEEN: How dare you question me! I should have you thrown in the dungeons to rot away!

RAMSBOTTOM: Sorry your Majesty.

QUEEN: I will shout for Snow White to come here. I will tell her that you're both going to the woods to find me some firewood, and once her back is turned… WHACK.

RAMSBOTTOM: Whack?

QUEEN: Yes, Whack. She. Is. Dead. *(Evil laugh)* Oh Snow White could you please come here!

(Enter SNOW WHITE)

Snow White, it's getting awfully cold in this castle. I need you to go out into the forest and collect me some firewood so we can fully stock the fires.

SNOW WHITE: But it's very dark outside.

QUEEN: Don't worry that's why I'm sending Ramsbottom with you, to keep you safe.

SNOW WHITE: Well, that's actually very kind of you

QUEEN: I know I'm feeling generous.

SNOW WHITE: I'll just go and get my coat *(Exit SNOW WHITE)*

QUEEN: Oh, and Ramsbottom, so I know the deed is done I wish for you to bring me Snow White's heart. Now be gone and do not return until Snow White is dead *(Evil Laugh)*

Song Four – QUEEN

(Exit QUEEN. MUDDLES and DAME MAISY appear from hiding places)

MUDDLES: Hiya Gang! *(Audience: Hiya Muddles)*

DAME: Did you hear that Muddles!

MUDDLES: I know! We've got to save Snow White and stop the Queen's evil plan!

DAME: Right, I'll tell you what we'll do, we'll follow Ramsbottom and Snow White into the forest to make sure no harm comes to Snow White.

MUDDLES: Sounds like a plan to me!

DAME: We'll take the horses!

MUDDLES: Where are the horses?

DAME: *(Points offstage)* Just over there in the distance.

MUDDLES: How comes they're not over here?

DAME: They weren't in the budget.

(Blackout)

SCENE FOUR
THE FOREST

(Enter SNOW WHITE followed by RAMSBOTTOM)

SNOW WHITE: I've never been this far into the forest before-

RAMSBOTTOM: No. Nobody could find us out here.

SNOW WHITE: Yes, it's very far.

(RAMSBOTTOM sits on a rock and starts to cry)

Whatever is the matter Ramsbottom? Why are you crying?

RAMSBOTTOM: That nasty, rotten, ugly old Queen sent me out here with you to kill you. But I can't do it, I couldn't kill anyone, I only went along with it because I was scared.

SNOW WHITE: Oh you poor man! Come here *(She gives him a hug)*. It'll be alright!

RAMSBOTTOM: I'm really sorry, I promise I'll be good from now on-

SNOW WHITE: But you were never bad in the first place! The Queen is the only baddie around here, I always thought she was a bit mean. But I never knew she was this mean!

RAMSBOTTOM: Oh, she's a proper baddie!

(DAME MAISY and MUDDLES come steaming in at full pace)

DAME: Stop! *(Jumping on RAMSBOTTOM)*

MUDDLES: Hiya Gang! *(Audience: Hiya Muddles)*. The game's up Ramsbottom!

SNOW WHITE: Stop! Stop! He hasn't done anything wrong!

DAME: *(Still wrestling with RAMSBOTTOM)* We heard all about the Queen's plan!

SNOW WHITE: Yes, Ramsbottom told me all about it and he's refused to go through with it!

DAME: *(Getting up and pulling RAMSBOTTOM to his feet and dusting him down)* Well, in that case then, my sincerest apologies!

MUDDLES: So, how comes you didn't do it!

RAMSBOTTOM: I'm just not a baddie, I couldn't hurt a fly let alone the lovely Snow White.

DAME: Well in that case then what are you going to tell the Queen when you get back?

RAMSBOTTOM: I can't go back!

DAME: You've got to go back. All of us have to otherwise the Queen will know something's up and Snow White's life will still be in danger!

MUDDLES: You know she's right.

SNOW WHITE: You don't all have to do this just for me.

MUDDLES: Nonsense Snow White I'd do anything for you.

SNOW WHITE: Oh Muddles, you've always been like a brother to me…

MUDDLES: Oh, but I love you Snow White-

SNOW WHITE: Like I sister I know.

MUDDLES: Yeah, like a sister.

RAMSBOTTOM: There's only one problem, that horrid Queen asked me to bring back the heart of Snow White to prove that I'd done the job properly.

DAME: Not to worry we had pig's heart for dinner the other night I'm sure there's still some leftovers in the kitchen you can have one of those, that nasty old Queen will never notice the difference!

MUDDLES: Hang on we had pigs' heart for dinner! You told me that was beef stew!

DAME: No what I said was eat up, this is a good hearty meal!

MUDDLES: Ergh!

DAME: I'm so sorry Snow White, but we'll have to leave you here in the forest. That way none of us know of your whereabouts, so if the Queen finds out we're lying we won't be able to tell her where you are.

RAMSBOTTOM: Here take this *(hands over a sat nav)*.

SNOW WHITE: What's this?

RAMSBOTTOM: It's a Sat Nav. It'll keep you on the right path, so you won't get lost.

SNOW WHITE: But how will you find your way back home?

RAMSBOTTOM: There's three of us-

MUDDLES: Yeah, and there's nothing scarier in this forest than my Mum!

DAME: Cheeky!

MUDDLES: Look after yourself Snow White!

DAME: We'll never forget you!

SNOW WHITE: Will I ever see any of you again?

DAME: Of course you will. I love you like you were my own.

MUDDLES: And remember if the love is true, we'll always see each other again!

(Exit MUDDLES, DAME MAISY and RAMSBOTTOM)

Song Five – SNOW WHITE & PRINCE FREDERICK *(Split scene).*

(Song Ends. Exit SNOW WHITE)

PRINCE: I've been wandering in this woodland for weeks now, ever since I was thrown into the forest by the Queen's guards. The only thing keeping me alive is the thought of seeing the beautiful Snow White again. I'll keep moving through the forest surviving off the land. I will find Snow White again and when I do, we'll get married and live happily ever after! *(Exit PRINCE)*

ACT 1   SNOW WHITE   31

SCENE FIVE

THE ROYAL PALACE

(Enter RAMSBOTTOM, DAME MAISY and MUDDLES)

MUDDLES: Hiya Gang! *(Audience: Hiya Muddles)*

DAME: It's good to be back! But I can't help but worry about Snow White out there in the forest.

MUDDLES: Don't worry Mum, she'll be fine. She's got the Sat Nav I'm sure she's safe and sound by now!

RAMSBOTTOM: I've always found shelter using that sat nav!

MUDDLES: I know what'll make us feel better, how about some chocolate!

(During this scene each time a chocolate bar is mentioned they hold up a picture of the chocolate bar)

DAME: Chocolate at a time like this? Hold on TIME OUT.

RAMSBOTTOM: Chocolate I thought you said we were having a PICNIC?

MUDDLES: Yeah, you can have ALL SORTS, at a picnic!

DAME: All sorts aren't a chocolate bar! Come on keep on TOPIC!

MUDDLES: Fine. Are we still going to BOURNVILLE to take a trip to CADBURY world?

DAME: We've got no transport it might as well be in another GALAXY. How do you suppose we get there?

RAMSBOTTOM: We could take a DOUBLE DECKER there.

MUDDLES: Or we could take an AERO plane.

DAME: Can you both speak up a bit I can barely hear you. It's like you're saying everything in a WISPA

RAMSBOTTOM: Sorry I'll try and BREAKAWAY from talking too quietly Sir!

DAME: Sir? I think you'll find I'm a woman, I prefer to be called HERSHEY *(Her-She)*.

MUDDLES: Yeah, try to be a bit less of a WONKA

RAMSBOTTOM: A beg your pardon.

MUDDLES: WONKA BAR

DAME: MM *(M&Ms)*. Don't worry kids your grown ups will explain that one at the end.

MUDDLES: Yeah, some of the grown ups look like a proper HAPPY HIPPO

DAME: You can't say that it's rude! For FUDGE sake!

RAMSBOTTOM: I think we're forgetting about the Queen. If she finds out we're lying she'll put a BOUNTY on our heads!

MUDDLES: Right, it's CRUNCH time. We need to come up with a plan.

DAME: Yes, this is no time to be LION around. Honestly Muddles sometimes I think you're on a different planet!

MUDDLES: What MARS?

RAMSBOTTOM: That's quite a trip round the MILKY WAY.

DAME: Well, you can't just become a DRIFTER travelling through space! Come back to Earth and let's think of a plan!

MUDDLES: Right calm down don't get your SNICKERS in a TWIX

DAME: I am calm, it's just this plan is a bit ROCKY

MUDDLES: Well, I think it'll work, which gives me a BOOST

RAMSBOTTOM: So, what is the plan SMARTIE pants?

DAME: No idea, but I'm off, I've got a date with a man from Turkey, he's a real TURKISH DELIGHT!

RAMSBOTTOM: He must like his women CHUNKY

MUDDLES: Yeah, and with their own set of *(Holds up the last picture of a chocolate bar; a NUTS chocolate bar)*

(Comedy Jingle. They all take a bow after the final chocolate bar)

DAME: Oh, I can't help but worry about Snow White all alone in that forest despite you saying that she has the sat nav and it'll keep her on the safest path-

RAMSBOTTOM: What if I told you there was a way you could see her and make sure she is safe?

MUDDLES: What do you mean?

ACT 1 — SNOW WHITE — 33

RAMSBOTTOM: The Queen has an all-powerful Magic Mirror that can give you the answer to anything and let you see anything you want?

MUDDLES: Anything?

DAME: Careful this is a family show!

MUDDLES: Well, where is this magic mirror?

RAMSBOTTOM: Right here! *(Unveils the magic mirror by opening the closet)*

MIRROR: I thought you'd never uncover me. I've been in the closet for ages!

DAME: Haven't we both dear.

RAMSBOTTOM: Don't you normally speak in rhyme?

MIRROR: Usually yes, but it gets so tedious. It's harder than you think talking in rhyme! You try it.

MUDDLES: *(Said as if thinking out loud)* I had a red-hot curry, Which got me moving in a hurry. My trousers started to split And suddenly I needed a-

DAME, RAMSBOTTOM & MIRROR: Muddles!

DAME: *(To MIRROR)* Can you show us Snow White?

MUDDLES: Yes, and show us that she's alright and safe?

MIRROR: I can indeed. *(The MIRROR waves his hands in a magical way and SNOW WHITE appears. This can be done behind a gauze or as a split scene)*

RAMSBOTTOM: See I told you the Sat Nav would help her stick to the safe path!

MUDDLES: This Mirror's amazing!

MIRROR: Thank you very much!

DAME: What else can you do?

MIRROR: Well let me show you! Music!

Song Six – MIRROR & CAST

(Song Ends)

MUDDLES: Wow that was amazing!

MIRROR: The Queen is coming!

DAME: How do you know?

MIRROR: I'm a magic walking talking mirror. I know everything!

DAME: Fair enough.

MUDDLES: You best get back in the closest Mr. erm what do we call you?

MIRROR: Just call me Magic Mirror or Mirror for short! *(Gets back in the closet and close the door)*

(Enter QUEEN with a Selfie Stick)

QUEEN: What are you all doing in here?

MUDDLES: We were pretending to be the 3 MUSKETEERS *(Holding up a picture of a '3 Musketeers' bar)*-

QUEEN: What?

MUDDLES: It's a chocolate bar in America... Never mind.

QUEEN: Muddles, Maisy.

MUDDLES & DAME: Yes, your majesty?

QUEEN: Get out. *(MUDDLES and DAME exit bowing as they leave)* Now Ramsbottom, tell me is Snow White dead?

RAMSBOTTOM: Yes, your majesty.

QUEEN: Now Ramsbottom, if Snow White is truly dead do you have her heart as promised.

RAMSBOTTOM: Yes, as promised your Majesty. I've left it in your bedroom for you to inspect.

QUEEN: You have done well Ramsbottom.

RAMSBOTTOM: Thank your Majesty.

QUEEN: You may leave. So, with Snow White dead I am back to being the most beautiful woman in the land!

Song Seven – QUEEN & STYLISTS

(Evil Laugh. Blackout.)

SCENE SIX

THE DWARFS COTTAGE

(The lights slowly fade up on the Dwarfs cottage, there is a sense of magic in the air, we wait a beat for SNOW WHITE to enter. SNOW WHITE is followed by woodland creatures who she plays with, they lead her into the cottage. She hits her head on the ceiling.)

SNOW WHITE: Ouch! My head! *(To the animals)* Thank you all so much for helping to find shelter, it was starting to get very cold. I wonder who lives here, seven beds and they're all very small and there's mining equipment and that's small as well and look on the beds there's seven very small night caps. I wonder who could live here? This is all rather strange. I'm so tired though I've been walking for hours, I think I'll have to have a little nap. *(SNOW WHITE lays down and goes to sleep. The animals put a blanket over SNOW WHITE and tuck her in, after they've done this they exit).*

(Suddenly we hear marching. The SEVEN DWARFS enter the stage marching carrying their tools from a hard day's work with them. The song happens in front of the cottage outside as does the dialogue between the Dwarfs)

Song Eight – *THE SEVEN DWARFS*

(Song Ends)

POP: Good days work today everyone!

JOLLY: *(Sings)* Hi-Ho-

POP: Jolly what have I told you about singing that do you want us to get sued?

JOLLY: Sorry, though I thought my name was Happy?

POP: Nope, nope… Not in this version!

JOLLY: Come to think of it aren't we supposed to be dwarfs?

WHEEZY: I mean I'm fairly short!

SURLY: Yes, but you're still not a dwarf! The audience looked so confused when we marched out!

POP: Look we all know the reason why we're not proper dwarfs-

DOZY: Is it because of a magical spell cast up on us?

SNOOZY: Oh, I know it's something to do with that beast living in the castle-

POP: The beast in the castle?

JOLLY: He's thinking of last year!

POP: No, the reason why we're not the right size is due to is erm… well… its…

DWARFS: *(To the audience)* Budget cuts.

POP: Well I'm glad we've cleared that up!

SNOOZY: *(Big Yawn)* well I'm going straight to bed!

WHEEZY: *(Sneezes)* And I'm going to make myself a lemsip!

SURLY: And I'm going to read the newspaper and don't anyone disturb me!

DOZY: And I'm going to… I don't know… Maybe I'll erm…

POP: And what about you Blusher, what will you do?

BLUSHER: *(Shrugs his shoulders)*

POP: Come on then, everyone in and I'll start dinner!

(JOLLY enters the cottage first and comes running back out)

JOLLY: There's someone inside the cottage!

POP: What do you mean?

JOLLY: I think it could be a monster!

POP: Okay then boys, we'll all go in together!

(The DWARFS all pick up there working tools and sneak into the cottage and surround a sleeping SNOW WHITE. Pop gives her a poke to wake her up. SNOW WHITE sits up the blanket covering her!

JOLLY: *(Screams)* it's a monster!

(SNOW WHITE takes the blanket off)

SNOOZY: *(Screams)* it's a girl!

(All of the DWARFS run and hide apart from POP)

SNOW WHITE: Oh, my goodness, hello! I hope I didn't startle you. My name's Snow White! And who are you?

ACT 1   SNOW WHITE

POP: It's alright everyone she's fine we're all safe. We're the seven Dwarfs-

SNOW WHITE: Dwarfs?

POP: Yes we know, we've been through all that already-

SNOW WHITE: But aren't dwarfs supposed to be small?

SMALLEST DWARF: *(Peering out from their hiding place)* Well, I'm short-

POP: Look, we're not doing this again. We're the seven dwarfs-

SNOW WHITE: Oh yes, I know; Sneezy, Bashful, Sleepy-

POP: *(Quickly interrupting)* Nope not those dwarfs! We live here in this cottage, and we work in the mines digging for diamonds. I'm Pop. Come on boys you can come out. Come on introduce yourselves don't be shy!

SNOOZY: *(Big yawn)* I'm Snoozy

JOLLY: I'm Jolly, a pleasure to meet you Snow White!

SURLY: Alright.

POP: That's Surly don't worry you'll get use to him!

WHEEZY: *(Sneezes)* I'm Wheezy! Nice to meet you, you wouldn't happen to have a cough drop on you, would you? *(Sneezes again)*

POP: It's only the pollen making him sneeze! Go and take an antihistamine for your hay fever!

BLUSHER: *(Waves timidly)*

POP: That's Blusher he's a little shy! Now Where's Snoozy? *(SNOOZY is already face down in his bed asleep)* Of course he's already asleep, he's not called Snoozy for no reason, he loves a snooze!

DOZY: *(Shakes SURLY'S hand)* Nice to meet you Snow White, I'm Dozy!

SURLY: Do I look like Snow White to you!

DOZY: *(Laughs)* Oh sorry! *(Goes over to SNOW WHITE)* Nice to meet you I'm Dozy!

SNOW WHITE: How wonderful to meet you all and sorry for coming into your home without asking, it's just it was getting dark and I'm on the run really…

POP: Who from?

SNOW WHITE: My stepmother the Wicked Queen!

POP: Well, you're welcome to stay with us, you might have to duck a bit in here. But we're happy to have you! Aren't we fellas?

DWARFS: Yeah, sure we are! More than welcome etc

SNOW WHITE: Thank you so much!

POP: We've heard horrible stories about that Queen, that's why we steer well clear of her and live all the way out here!

JOLLY: Yeah, we heard she's mean and nasty

SNOW WHITE: She is! She's been particularly nasty to me! She tried to have me killed

(The DWARFS gasp in horror)

JOLLY: Well, you're safe with us here!

POP: And like I said you can stay as long as you want!

Song Nine – SNOW WHITE & THE SEVEN DWARFS

(End of Act One)

ACT TWO
SCENE ONE
THE DIAMOND MINE

Song Ten – SNOW WHITE & THE SEVEN DWARFS

(Song Ends)

SNOW WHITE: My goodness no wonder you all come home so tired! You all work so hard!

POP: Nothing like a good day's work to build up an appetite!

SNOW WHITE: Now what would you all like for your dinner?

POP: You don't have to cook for us all every night Snow White!

JOLLY: Yeah, why don't we cook for you!

SNOW WHITE: Very well if you insist! What are you making me?

POP: Well, we've got some mini quiches!

DOZY: Some mini fillet burgers!

JOLLY: Mini cupcakes!

WHEEZY: And some midget gems!

SURLY: Those jokes would work a lot better if we were actually dwarfs!

POP: Okay, Surly don't get your knickers in a twist, we're just having some fun!

SURLY: I guess I'm just a bit tired

SNOOZY: Me too!

SURLY: You're always tired!

SNOOZY: That's probably why they call me Snoozy!

DOZY: I thought I was called Snoozy?

SURLY: No you're Dozy!

DOZY: Oh yeah! I guess I forgot!

SNOW WHITE: I'll tell you what, why don't I make dinner tonight and you can all prepare me something tomorrow!

JOLLY: Oh Snow White you do look after us!

SNOW WHITE: It's my pleasure! I'll tell you what, you all set up ready for dinner and I'll go and get it!

(The DWARFS all set for dinner with little tables and chairs. SNOW WHITE comes back on with a trolley of food and serves each Dwarf individually)

SNOW WHITE: Now let's see for Pop, we've got Steak, chips and egg *(Places the food down)*.

POP: Thanks!

SNOW WHITE: Surely, we've got ham, egg and chips, one egg fried and one scrambled.

SURLY: This looks delicious!

SNOW WHITE: Jolly, a roast dinner with beef and plenty of roast potatoes all served in a giant Yorkshire pudding.

JOLLY: Amazing, thanks Snow White!

SNOW WHITE: Wheezy, we've got fish and chips with plenty of salt and vinegar! And of course no pepper!

WHEEZY: *(Sneezes. SNOW WHITE hands him a handkerchief)*. Thanks!

SNOW WHITE: Dozy, you've got a chicken stir fry with extra chicken chunks.

DOZY: Gee thanks Snow White!

SNOW WHITE: Snoozy, a full English with a side of onion rings.

SNOOZY: I've been thinking about this all day!

SNOW WHITE: And finally Blusher, eggs and soldiers and plenty of tomato sauce as well

BLUSHER: *(Smiles)*

SNOW WHITE: And for me a big full English breakfast with a side of steak, ham, spam, eggs, onion rings, French fries, olives, nachos with plenty of chilli and cheese, a bowl of cereal, peanut butter on toast and ice cream for dessert to finish it all off!

(THE DWARFS all look up from their plates in disbelief at how much SNOW WHITE has)

I've worked hard as well you know! *(She Smiles)*. Come on everyone, let's eat!

ACT 2   SNOW WHITE   41

SCENE TWO

THE ROYAL PALACE

(Enter RAMSBOTTOM & MUDDLES)

MUDDLES: Hiya Gang! *(Audience Hiya Muddles)*. Mum, I'm really hungry!

RAMSBOTTOM: How come we've not long eaten!

MUDDLES: Maybe we could have some Ice cream?

RAMSBOTTOM: Ice cream? Ice Cream?

MUDDLES: *(Sung)* Just one cornetto…

RAMSBOTTOM: *(Sung)* …Give it to me!

MUDDLES: *(Sung)* You must be joking they're £3.50!

RAMSBOTTOM: Right fine we can have some ice cream… If you sing me a song about ice cream!

MUDDLES: But I don't know any songs about ice cream!

RAMSBOTTOM: Well, I'm sure you can make one up.

MUDDLES: Alright I will. And when I've finished the song, will I get it?

RAMSBOTTOM: Get what?

MUDDLES: The ice cream!

RAMSBOTTOM: Oh yes, you'll get it alright, a lovely big plate of it!

MUDDLES: You promise?

RAMSBOTTOM: Oh yes! You start singing and I'll go and get it! *(Exit DAME)*

MUDDLES: Could I have some Ice Cream music please!

Song Eleven (A) – Ice Cream Song - MUDDLES

Ice Cream, Ice Cream I like lots of Ice Cream
I don't like kippers and I don't like ham
I don't like bread and I don't like jam
I'll have it for my supper, I'll have it for my tea
So, if you have some ice cream, please give it to me!

(RAMSBOTTOM puts a plate of ice cream into MUDDLES face at the end of the song)

MUDDLES: *(Wiping cream away from his face)* You've put it right in my face! Hold on this ice cream tastes funny!

RAMSBOTTOM: Yes, it's Gillette. It's the best ice cream a man can get!

MUDDLES: Hang on here comes Mum, do you think she'd like some Ice Cream?

RAMSBOTTOM: You'll have to ask her

(Enter DAME)

MUDDLES: Hello Mum, would you like some Ice Cream?

DAME: Ice cream, why yes of course I would!

MUDDLES: Well all you have to do is sing a song about Ice Cream

DAME: But, I don't know a song about Ice cream-

MUDDLES: Don't worry Ramsbottom can help you sing it! Won't you?

RAMSBOTTOM: Oh, no problem at all!

DAME: And then I'll get it?

MUDDLES: Oh, you'll get it alright

Song Eleven (B) – Ice Cream Song – RAMSBOTTOM & DAME

RAMSBOTTOM & DAME:

Ice Cream, Ice Cream I like lots of Ice Cream
I don't like kippers and I don't like ham
I don't like bread and I don't like jam
I'll have it for my supper, I'll have it for my tea
So, if you have some ice cream, please give it to me!

(On the last line of the song DAME puts her hands out and unknowingly knocks the ice cream into MUDDLES face, he quickly gathers himself before DAME sees she's had the ice cream knocked in his face)

DAME: I didn't even get any ice cream!

RAMSBOTTOM: Why not try it faster? *(Shouting to MUDDLES)* Are you ready this time?

MUDDLES: *(From offstage)* Oh yes he'll get a lovely big plate of it this time!

DAME: And I should do it faster this time?

MUDDLES: *(From Offstage)* You'll get your ice cream quicker if you do!

DAME: Very well, music please but this time twice as fast!

(This time the song is a quicker version. When DAME sings the song this time MUDDLES runs on at speed trips over and puts the plate of ice cream in his own face. He quickly goes offstage before DAME notices he has put the plate of ice cream in his face again)

Song Eleven (C) – Ice Cream Song (Sped Up Version) – DAME

Ice Cream, Ice Cream I like lots of Ice Cream
I don't like kippers and I don't like ham
I don't like bread and I don't like jam
I'll have it for my supper, I'll have it for my tea
So, if you have some ice cream, please give it to me!

DAME: Still no ice cream?

RAMSBOTTOM: I'll tell you what, I'll go and get some ice cream as well and then you'll definitely get it!

DAME: Will I?

RAMSBOTTOM: Yes, sing it one more time and then this time you'll definitely get it!

DAME: You're sure?

RAMSBOTTOM: Oh yes! *(Exit RAMSBOTTOM)*

DAME: Very well then. Music please!

Song Eleven (D) – Ice Cream Song - DAME

Ice Cream, Ice Cream I like lots of Ice Cream
I don't like kippers and I don't like ham
I don't like bread and I don't like jam
I'll have it for my supper, I'll have it for my tea
So, if you have some ice cream, please give it to me!

(At the end of the song this time both RAMSBOTTOM and MUDDLES have a plate of ice cream, as the they go to put them in DAME'S face she manages to duck out of the way and RAMSBOTTOM and MUDDLES end up putting ice cream in each others face. DAME looks at both RAMSBOTTOM and

MUDDLES who are both covered in ice cream)
DAME: Do you know I think I'll have a lolly instead!
(Blackout)

SCENE THREE
THE ROYAL PALACE

QUEEN: *(Evil Laugh)* Did you miss me? Wait a second I can feel an Insta post coming on *(takes out her phone for a selfie)*, can we get the lights in her to make me look even more beautiful than I already am? *(Blackout)* Everyone's a comedian. Turn the lights back on now! *(Lights Up)* With Snow White dead I am now the most beautiful woman in the land. Snow White is dead and gone! Oh yes she is!

(AUDIENCE: oh no she's not!)

Oh yes she is!

(AUDIENCE: oh no she's not!)

Oh yes she is!

(AUDIENCE: oh no she's not!).

Oh, shut up you pathetic lot… Hang on, Snow White's alive? I can just check with my Magic Mirror! Mirror reveal yourself!

MIRROR: Yes, your majesty?

QUEEN: Mirror, mirror on the wall, who's the fairest of them all?

MIRROR: Not you. It's still Snow White

QUEEN: Snow White's alive? How can it be? Ramsbottom! Get in here this instance!

RAMSBOTTOM: Yes, your majesty.

QUEEN: My magic mirror tells me that Snow White is still alive. But you told me that she was dead! You lied to me Ramsbottom!

RAMSBOTTOM: I'm sorry your majesty I just couldn't go through with it!

QUEEN: Guards! *(Enter the QUEENS GUARDS)* Take Ramsbottom to the Dungeon lock him in and throw away the key!

(RAMSBOTTOM is dragged off by the GUARDS)

HONESTLY IF YOU WANT A JOB DOING properly you may as well do it yourself! *(Picks up a spell book)* Guards bring me my cauldron! *(GUARDS bring on a cauldron centre stage. Exit*

GUARDS.) What I'll do using powerful magic is create a poisoned apple and then I'll trick Snow White in to eating it, one bite and she'll be dead!

(Begins to flick through the spell book) Now where is that delightful spell... Ah! here we are, a poisoned apple for eternal rest! Hang on there's some small print here; the spell of eternal rest can only be broken by love. Ha! Love! Like anyone will ever love Snow White! *(Evil Laugh)*

MIRROR: You can't do that to Snow White, she's done nothing wrong!

QUEEN: Shut up you over blown piece of glass! Be gone Mirror and leave me be!

(Exit MIRROR)

Now where was I? Ah yes here we go!
Tail of a rat and eyes of a newt
To help us make this devious fruit!
Venom of a snake all aid in deceit
Ought to help make the spell complete
Liver of a cat and frog spawn too
And eyes of a bat to see this through
Dip the apple in the poison brew
And make sure your victim has a good chew

(The QUEEN pulls out the poison apple from the cauldron)

Now I have the poison apple, I'll need a disguise. I'll turn myself into a trusting old hag and trick that stupid girl Snow White into taking a bite of the poisoned apple! Now to turn myself into a hag I'll need even more powerful magic!

Song Twelve – QUEEN & MINIONS (During this number the QUEEN transforms into an old hag)

(Song ends with the QUEEN now the Old Hag centre giving an evil laugh holding the poisoned apple)

ACT 2   SNOW WHITE   47

SCENE FOUR
THE ROYAL PALACE

(Enter DAME followed by MUDDLES and a chorus of school children)

DAME: Right come on now boys and girls it's time for school!

MUDDLES: Mum do I have to go to school?

DAME: Yes, and why shouldn't you?

MUDDLES: Because I'm a *(enter real age here)* year old man!

DAME: Oh, be quiet Muddles and join the rest of the class! Now it's time for a pop quiz!

ALL: *(Moan, 'do we have too' etc)*

DAME: Yes, we do! Now who wants to answer the first question?

MUDDLES: *(Trying to get DAME's attention)* Psst!

DAME: I most certainly am not! Now Muddles answer me this; which battle was Nelson killed?

MUDDLES: His last one

DAME: Correct. What's E.T short for?

CHILD 1: *(Stands up)* He's only got little legs.

DAME: Correct. What caused the trouble in the garden of Eden was it the apple on the tree-

MUDDLES: *(Stands up)* No, it was the pair on the ground.

DAME: Correct. What is red and smells like blue paint?

CHILD 2: Red paint

DAME: Correct. Where does a general keep his armies?

CHILD 3: Up his sleevies!

DAME: Correct. Why does a Squirrel swim on his back?

MUDDLES: To keep his nuts dry.

DAME: Correct. What do you call bears with no ears?

CHILD 4: B

DAME: Correct. What's a foot long and slippery?

CHILD 5: A slipper

DAME: Where is the most desolate place on earth?

CHILD 1: Jaywick

DAME: Correct. What's red and moves up and down?

CHILD 2: A tomato in an elevator.

DAME: Correct. Who was born in a stable and worshipped by millions?

CHILD 3: Red Rum

DAME: Correct. If you have four chocolate bars in one hand, three chocolate bars in the other hand and you've already eaten three. What have you got?

MUDDLES: Diabetes.

DAME: Correct. What's- *(buzzer sounds to indicate the end of the round)* I've started so I'll finish; What's the difference between an oral thermometer and a rectal thermometer?

MUDDLES: The taste.

DAME: Correct. Now it's almost time for dinner!

MUDDLES: Can we change the school cook?

CHORUS: Yes, change the cook etc

DAME: Why do you want to change the school cook?

MUDDLES: Well, the beef wellington tasted like actual wellingtons, the cottage pie tasted like a cottage, and as for the spotted dick-

DAME: Thank you Muddles! Now if everybody could look at the board. *(Notices someone has written 'BNAG' on the board)* It looks as though some has been vandalising my board again!

MUDDLES: Oh, that's bang out of order!

DAME: Yes, thank you Muddles! Now let's start with-

MUDDLES: *(Puts his hand up)* Miss! Oh Miss! Miss!

DAME: Yes Muddles, what is it?

MUDDLES: Can I go to the toilet?

DAME: No, you can wait like everyone else!

ACT 2 — SNOW WHITE

49

MUDDLES: But I really need to go!

DAME: Fine, you can go to the toilet if you recite the alphabet as quickly as you can!

MUDDLES: Fine, no problem. A, B, C, D, E, F, G, H, I, J, K, L, M, N, O, Q, R, S, T, U, V, W, X, Y, Z.

DAME: Hang on where's the P gone?

MUDDLES: I think it's running down my leg!

(School bell rings. Enter MIRROR in a hurry)

MIRROR: I need your help, well Snow White needs your help!

DAME: Is she in danger?

MIRROR: Yes, that horrible Queen found out that Snow White is still alive and she's thrown Ramsbottom in the dungeon and thrown away the key!

MUDDLES: That's terrible!

MIRROR: And that's not even the worst part. She's planning to kill Snow White with a poisoned apple!

MUDDLES: But surely Snow White will spot the Queen coming from a mile off!

MIRROR: No, she won't. You see the Queen has used powerful magic to disguise herself as an old hag!

DAME & MUDDLES: Oh no!

DAME: What can we do?

MIRROR: Well first of all you need to break Ramsbottom out of the dungeon, as he can help you navigate through the forest. Then you need to find Snow White before the Queen does!

DAME: Well, there's no time to lose! Come on Muddles, let's go!

(Exit DAME & MUDDLES)

MIRROR: Will Snow White be saved
Will the evil Queen learn how to behave?
Will I continue you to rhyme?
I might as well I've got some time!
We'll get that Queen, who's nasty and rotten
We'll see that love and bravery are never forgotten

So go on, go forth and be brave
It's Snow White you'll be needing to save!

(Blackout)

SCENE FIVE
THE FOREST

MUDDLES: Hiya gang! *(Audience: Hiya Muddles!)*

RAMSBOTTOM: We've been walking for ages, this is so much easier with my sat nav- Where even are we?

MUDDLES: Gets out a map, well let's see first of all we went this way underground

RAMSBOTTOM: Yes, then we came out and went overground?

MUDDLES: Then we bumped into that creature that helped point us in the right direction

RAMSBOTTOM: I remember that, strange creature. He asked for all of our rubbish as well, said he would make good use of the things that we gave him.

MUDDLES: Yes, in fact he said he'd make good use of things that he'd found. What was his name?

RAMSBOTTOM: I think it was Uncle Bulgaria.

DAME: So, let me get this straight. We've been underground. Overground. Wombling free?

(SFX comedy sting)

MUDDLES: I'm soooo tired!

DAME: Me too, but we've not got much of act two to go… I mean, that's because we've been walking for ages and we're lost.

RAMSBOTTOM: We're not lost!

MUDDLES: Then what are we?

RAMSBOTTOM: Diverted!

DAME: And it's starting to get dark.

(Sound effect of something falling and hitting the floor and the lights go dark)

RAMSBOTTOM: What was that?

MUDDLES: Nights fallen!

RAMSBOTTOM: Oh, I don't like it when it gets dark!

DAME: Me either!

MUDDLES: Yeah, I've heard that this forest is haunted!

DAME & RAMSBOTTOM: Haunted! *(They grab one another)*

MUDDLES: Yeah, by ghosties and ghoulies!

RAMSBOTTOM: Oh, I'd hate to be grabbed by the ghosties!

MUDDLES: And I'd hate to be grabbed by the ghoul- ghosties as well!

DAME: I'll tell you what, why don't we sing a song to calm us down and this lot out here will tell us if they see anything spooky! Won't you boys and girls! *(Ad lib as needed)*

Song Fourteen – DAME, MUDDLES & RAMSBOTTOM

(As they sing a GHOST enters the stage and waves around behind the cast onstage)

DAME, MUDDLES & RAMSBOTTOM: There was a what? *(Audience: a ghost!)* A ghost? Are you sure? *(Audience: Yes!)* Where did he go? (Audience: That way) Which way? This way? *(Audience: Yes)* Well, we'll have to have a look then! *(DAME, RAMSBOTTOM & MUDDLES all sneak round together in a line and the ghost joins the end of the line and scares RAMSBOTTOM who run off being chased by the ghost)*

DAME: Oh!! Where's Ramsbottom gone? *(Audience: the ghost got him!)* the ghost got him?

DAME & MUDDLES: Well, we'll have to sing it again then won't we! Whoops!

Song Fourteen (A) – DAME & MUDDLES

(As they sing a GHOST enters the stage and waves around behind the cast onstage)

DAME & MUDDLES: There was a what? *(Audience: a ghost!)* A ghost? Are you sure? *(Audience: Yes!)* Where did he go? *(Audience: That way)* Which way? This way? *(Audience: Yes)* Well, we'll have to have a look then! *(DAME & MUDDLES all sneak round together in a line and the GHOST joins the end of the line and scares MUDDLES who runs off being chased by the ghost)*

DAME: Oh!! Where's Muddles gone? *(Audience: the ghost got him!)* the ghost got him?

DAME: Well, I'll have to sing it again then won't I! Whoops!

Song Fourteen (B) – DAME

(As they sing a GHOST enters the stage and waves around behind DAME onstage)

DAME: There was a what? *(Audience: a ghost!)* A ghost? Are you sure? *(Audience: Yes!)* Where did he go? *(Audience: That way)* Which way? This way? *(Audience: Yes)* Well, I'll have to have a look then! *(DAME sneaks round and the GHOST joins DAME holding her hand as the sneak around the stage together. The ghost sneaks off before he's spotted)*

DAME: There's nothing there! Oh no there isn't! *(Audience: Oh yes there is!)*, Oh no there isn't! *(Audience: Oh yes there is!)*, Oh no there isn't! *(Audience: Oh yes there is!)*. Look there's absolutely no ghost here at all I think you're all being incredibly silly, playing tricks on me pretending there's a ghost there! Hang on are you all definitely sure there was a ghost? *(Audience: Yes!)* Are you sure? *(Audience: Yes!)* Well, I'll have to sing it again then won't I! Whoops!

Song Fourteen (C) – DAME

(As she sings a GHOST enters the stage and sits down next to her. DAME stops singing and looks at the GHOST they look back and forth at each other three times until the GHOST screams and runs off)

DAME: Charming!

(Blackout)

SCENE SIX
THE DWARFS COTTAGE

(SNOW WHITE is sat with the DWARFS finishing telling them a story from a story book)

SNOW WHITE: …And they all lived happily ever after!

JOLLY: Tell us another story Snow White

SNOW WHITE: Maybe I'll tell you the story of Beauty and the Beast next time!

SURLY: Beauty and the Beast? That's so last year!

DOZY: Oh, go on please Snow White, I love hearing your stories!

SNOW WHITE: I'd love to but I think Pop would like you all to start work at some point today!

POP: She's right there's still loads of diamonds to be mined

WHEEZY: *(Goes to sneeze)* A-choo! *(SNOW WHITE hands him a handkerchief)* Thank you Snow White!

SNOW WHITE: I'll make sure that dinner is ready for when you get in, and Surly-

SURLY: What?

SNOW WHITE: I've pack you a thermos of hot cocoa for work today. I know it's your favourite!

SURLY: Thanks!

SNOW WHITE: And Jolly I've made you sandwiches with the crusts cut off how you like!

JOLLY: Wow! Thanks Snow White!

SNOW WHITE: Blusher, I've made sure you have a big flask of tea with four sugars!

BLUSHER: *(Gives a timid thumbs up)*

SNOW WHITE: Dozy I've made sure that you've got a really bright torch for when you go down the mines, so you don't trip over again!

DOZY: Gee, thanks Snow White!

SNOW WHITE: And snoozy I've done you extra strong coffee to get you through the day!

SNOOZY: *(Lets out a big yawn)* Thanks!

SNOW WHITE: And finally Pop, the leader of the group, for you I've made some new shoes as I'd noticed your ones had some holes in, which can't have been very comfortable at all! Now have a good day at work all of you!

POP: Come on then boys, let's go to work! See you later Snow White

DWARFS: Bye Snow White, See you later etc

(Exit DWARFS. Enter QUEEN in disguise as the old hag)

QUEEN: It's me in disguise and I'm ready to trick Snow White *(evil laugh)*. One bite of this apple and she'll drop down to the floor, dead! And then I'll be the most beautiful woman in the land! *(Evil laugh)*. Here comes Snow White now, you lot keep your mouths shut and don't say a word while I trick her with fatal consequences! *(As the old hag)* Hello deary

SNOW WHITE: Oh, you startled me!

QUEEN: I didn't mean to startle you my dear, in fact I come here only to help you!

SNOW WHITE: How will you help me?

QUEEN: Well, I've been wandering these forests picking the nicest juiciest apples. They're so scrumptious, but I have no friends to share them with...

SNOW WHITE: Well, that's very sad-

QUEEN: Unless you'd like an apple my dear?

SNOW WHITE: Oh, I don't know if I should

QUEEN: Of course you should! *(Takes a shiny red apple)*. I saved this one just for a pretty girl like you!

SNOW WHITE: Very well *(takes the apple)*. I'll save it for later

QUEEN: No! *(Calms herself)*. I want to see you enjoy the apple and tell me how sweet and delicious it is...

SNOW WHITE: What do you think boys and girls can I trust this lady? *(ad lib as needed)*

QUEEN: Of course you can trust me!

SNOW WHITE: You look fairly trustworthy to me!

QUEEN: Go on just one bite!

SNOW WHITE: *(Goes to bite the apple)* You're sure this will be the best apple I've ever tasted?

QUEEN: Yes, yes go on! Eat it, take a bite!

SNOW WHITE: Alright *(she takes a bite)*. Oh, I feel rather strange. *(She begins to wobble. She collapses on the floor)*

QUEEN: At last Snow White is dead! *(Evil laugh)* And there's nothing any of you horrible little brats can do about it! *(Evil laughter.)*

Song Fifteen – QUEEN

(The song finishes. Blackout)

SCENE SEVEN
THE DWARFS COTTAGE

(SNOW WHITE is laid on a bed surrounded by flowers and the SEVEN DWARFS. Enter DAME, MUDDLES and RAMSBOTTOM)

MUDDLES: Oh no we're too late!

SURLY: Who are you lot!

DAME: Who are we? Who are you? And what are you doing with Snow White?

POP: Look everybody just calm down. I'm Pop and Snow White was living with us after she ran away from that evil Queen. We're her friends. Well… Were her friends.

RAMSBOTTOM: What can we do? The spell the Queen used to poison the apple was incredibly powerful!

DAME: Love! Love Is the answer.

POP: It's true love can break any evil spell for love conquers all!

(Enter PRINCE, he is now dressed in rags as if he's been living in the forest for months)

DAME: Oh, my goodness! Who are you?

PRINCE: It's me Prince Frederick, sorry I look such a state I've been living in the forest these past few months ever since I refused to marry the Queen and she banished me out into the forest! Tell me, what has happened to Snow White?

POP: She's been poisoned by that Evil Queen.

RAMSBOTTOM: And only love can bring her back!

PRINCE: Well looks like I've arrived just in time, when me and Snow White met, I knew it was love at first site! Maybe a kiss will wake her from her eternal slumber.

DAME: It's worth a shot!

MUDDLES: I hope this works!

(PRINCE kisses SNOW WHITE and she awakens)

SNOW WHITE: What happened? *(Noticing PRINCE FREDERICK)* Frederick! *(They kiss)*

PRINCE: You were poisoned by the Queen, but fortunately our love was strong enough to break the evil spell.

DAME: Hang on if Snow White is alive and well again, surely the Queen will find out and we'll all be in danger!

PRINCE: The there's only one thing to do, we must go back to the Palace and stand up to that Queen once and for all! Who's with me?

MUDDLES: I don't know she's very scary!

PRINCE: There's safety in numbers, all of us against her. We can't lose!

DAME: But how will we get back to the Palace from here?

SNOW WHITE: I still have the sat nav Ramsbottom gave me

RAMSBOTTOM: You're welcome.

SNOW WHITE: I'll set the destination and we can follow it all the way to the palace! Come on everyone follow me!

(Blackout)

SCENE EIGHT
THE ROYAL PALACE

QUEEN: *(She is now back to her normal self)* It's so good to be the fairest in all of the land again! Don't you just love me? *(Evil laugh)* Magic Mirror reveal yourself!

(Enter MIRROR)

MIRROR: Yes, your majesty?

QUEEN: Mirror, mirror on the wall, who's the fairest of them all?

MIRROR: Not you today or tonight,
The beauty of the land is Snow White!

QUEEN: WHAT?! How can that dreadful brat still be alive! I killed her myself! I poisoned her with the apple!

MIRROR: You did but it's only magic,
And not all spells need be tragic

QUEEN: Spit it out and talk properly, you stupid one-way window!

MIRROR: Love can break any evil spell. I mean you must have known that! Love conquers evil every time. But you were so wrapped up with being the best looking in the land you forgot to check the rules!

QUEEN: What rules?

MIRROR: I just told you love can break any evil spell.

QUEEN: But Snow White can't possibly be in love-

MIRROR: You forgot about Prince Frederick who you banished to the forest, it was love that kept him alive, and ultimately love that broke your evil spell! Love always wins!

QUEEN: Silence I need to think of a new plan! And this time it'll be the end of Snow White!

(Bursting into the scene at great pace; SNOW WHITE, followed by DAME, MUDDLES, RAMSBOTTOM, PRINCE and the SEVEN DWARFS)

SNOW WHITE: Not so fast! You won't be getting the best of me again!

QUEEN: You horrible little girl! And you've brought some ugly garden gnomes with you as well!

SURLY: Who are you calling gnomes!

QUEEN: Shut up all of you! Guards! Guards! Guards! *(No guards appear)*

DAME: You won't find any of your guards to come to your rescue!

MUDDLES: Yeah, we've locked them all in the dungeon!

QUEEN: How?

MUDDLES: We tricked them, they're actually surprisingly stupid!

SNOW WHITE: So that's it. The games up!

MIRROR: I told you, you were going to get your comeuppance!

QUEEN: Shut up you stupid bargain basement mirror! *(The QUEEN smashes the mirror)*

MIRROR: You've broken the mirror! I'm free! I'm free! If my mirror is ever broken it means that I am free and no longer a slave to the mirror.

QUEEN: Well good news for you!

MIRROR: And the person who breaks the mirror is to trade places with me!

QUEEN: Wait, what?! I didn't mean to break the mirror! You can't do this to me!

Song Sixteen – FULL CAST

(The QUEEN is banished to the mirror during the song)

PRINCE: Now there's just one last thing to do! Snow White will you marry me?

SNOW WHITE: Yes of course I will!

ALL: *(Cheer)*

RAMSBOTTOM: How about we make it a double whammy! Dame Maisy, will you marry me?

DAME: You want to marry me?

RAMSBOTTOM: You look surprised!

DAME: Not half as surprised as you'll look on our wedding night!

ALL: *(Cheer)*

(Tabs close and MUDDLES steps forward in front of the tabs)

ACT 2   SNOW WHITE   61

SCENE NINE
IN FRONT OF TABS

MUDDLES: Hiya Gang! Have you all had a good time? *(Audience: Yeah!)* Good I'm glad you've all enjoyed yourselves. But do you know I've always like Christmas though with it's presents and all it's songs! I've got a song about Christmas, would you like to hear it?

Song (Routine) Seventeen – 12 Days of Christmas – MUDDLES, DAME & RAMSBOTTOM

MUDDLES: Well, that was fun! Hang on a minute I might as well do it one last time! Hiya Gang! *(Audience: Hiya Muddles!)*. Now let's see I think we've got a few shout outs and birthdays to celebrate *(ad lib any announcements and birthdays. If there are any birthdays sing 'Happy Birthday')*

DAME: Is that singing I can hear? I do love a good sing song. I feel it really clears the cobwebs away!

MUDDLES: If you start singing you'll clear everyone away!

DAME: Oh I can't believe it, a happy ending!

MUDDLES: Snow White and Prince Frederick are getting married

DAME: And we'll never have to see that nasty old Queen again!

DAME: I'm so happy I could sing a song!

MUDDLES: Well that's handy because we know one!

DAME: Do we? Well isn't that a stroke of luck!

MUDDLES: Music please!

Song Eighteen – MUDDLES & DAME – Jelly on a Plate (Song sheet)

Jelly on the plate Jelly on the plate
Wibble wobble, wibble wobble Jelly on the plate
 Pancake in a pan Pancake in a pan
Flip it over, flip it over Pancake in a pan
Noodles on a fork Noodles on a fork
Twirly whirly, Twirly whirly Noodles on a fork

DAME: Oh that was so good Muddles!

MUDDLES: It was but I reckon everyone should join in!

DAME: Right then everyone on your feet!

MUDDLES: And just to make sure you're all joining in we've had the words written up nice and big so you can all see them! *(the song sheet descends from the top of the stage)*

DAME: Right then altogether, nice and loud! Music please!

Song Eighteen (A) – song sheet - MUDDLES & DAME

DAME: Now that was good! But I think this side were louder!

MUDDLES: Well that's funny because I thought this side, my side, were louder!

DAME: Well I tell you what, how about a bit of a competition, my side will go first and then yours afterwards

MUDDLES: But who can we get to judge it?

(RAMSBOTTOM enters)

RAMSBOTTOM: I'll do it!

DAME: What do you reckon everyone, should we let him do it? *(Audience: Yes!) (Ad lib as needed)*

MUDDLES: Right okay then we have our judge, you go first!

DAME: Very well, right, my side here we go!

Song Eighteen (B) – song sheet - DAME

MUDDLES: It was good, however my side let's do it even louder! *(Ad lib as needed)*

Song Eighteen (C) – sonbg sheet - MUDDLES

DAME: So, who's the winner?

MUDDLES: Yeah who's the winner?

RAMSBOTTOM: I have come to my decision and the winner is… This side! *(Pick whichever side was the loudest) (DAME and MUDDLES ad lib to whatever the decision is)*

DAME: Right well I've got a wedding to get ready for I'll see you later on! Bye for now! *(To RAMSBOTTOM)* Come on you! *(DAME and RAMSBOTTOM exit)*

MUDDLES: Well, I guess that just leaves us then! I'll tell you what let's sing it all together one last time, but this time the loudest you've ever sung it!

Song Eighteen (D) – song sheet - MUDDLES

MUDDLES: See you at the wedding! Bye *(Exit MUDDLES)*

(Tabs open for bows)

(BOWS)

MIRROR: I'm no longer trapped in that mirror on the wall

RAMSBOTTOM: I have a wife, she's like me both broad and tall

QUEEN: I'm stuck forever I should have been nice

POP: Yes, you really should have thought twice

SNOW WHITE: Prince Frederick and I are married and happy

PRINCE: I hope you didn't find this love story to sappy

DAME: Me and Ramsbottom will be alright

MUDDLES: This is the last thing I'll say tonight

SNOW WHITE: So, whether you've come from far or near

ALL: We hope to see you all next year!

Song Nineteen – Finale – All – Celebration

(Final Cast Bow)

(CURTAIN)

(END)

Also by Joe Meloy and available from Beercott Books

Set in the quaint little French village of [INSERT LOCAL REFERENCE HERE!], not far from [ANOTHER LOCAL REFERENCE!] is where our tale is set. Will the Beast be able to find true love before it's too late, will our dastardly villain Lucas Luxuriant get his comeuppance? Will Fairy Dust help save the day, and will Potty Pierre and Madame Marie Macaroon be able to get dinner ready and keep the Beast from going feral? Find out in this Pantomime adventure packed with fantastic gags, slapstick and something for all the family!

Jump into the rabbit hole and join Alice in Wonderland! How mad is the Mad Hatter? Will the White Rabbit ever be on time? Did anyone actually steal the Queen of Hearts jam tarts? Alice meets Duchess Dolly Dollop and Wally the White Rabbit, as they guide Alice through Wonderland and round up all of their friends to take on the Evil Queen of Hearts and save Wonderland!

About the author

I'm Joe Meloy ('...the excellent pantomime dame...' British Theatre Guide) and I'm an Actor, Pantomime Dame, Producer and Panto Enthusiast. I attended my first Pantomime when I was three and instantly fell in love with one of the most entertaining forms of theatre, in my humble opinion of course!

I have been performing in pantomime myself for a number of years having played Widow Twankey to an Ugly Sister, there have been one or two occasions where I haven't been in the dress, but I much prefer putting on my dresses, fake eyelashes and lip stick!

I performed my first professional Pantomime at twenty-three years old playing an Ugly Sister in an adult pantomime. I returned the next year to perform as Widow Twankey, from there I went on to play in family pantomimes as; Widow Twankey (twice more!) Dame Dolly Dollop, Nurse Nellie, King Arthur and as Maid Joan for the Hazlitt Theatre.

www.ingramcontent.com/pod-product-compliance
Lightning Source LLC
Chambersburg PA
CBHW042121100526
44587CB00025B/4137